Creative Cards

Picture Cards and Activities For English Language Development

Karen M. Sanders

Illustrated by Ross M. Sanders

Dominie Press, Inc.

Creative Cards

Publisher: Raymond Yuen
Executive Editor: Carlos A. Byfield
Editors: Bob Rowland & Becky Colgan
Designer: Carol Anne Craft

Published by

Dominie Press, Inc.

1949 Kellogg Avenue
Carlsbad, California 92008 USA

ISBN: 0-7685-0459-7

Printed in Singapore by PH Productions Pte. Ltd.
1 2 3 4 5 6 IP 01 00 99

Creative Cards

This book is dedicated to our parents,
who have always believed in us.
Thank you.

Acknowledgments

I would like to thank Karin Van der Auwera and Jo Sanders, two fellow teachers who gave me both the inspiration and the confidence to pursue this project. Thanks, too, to the staff and students of the Anchorage Literacy Project for all their feedback and encouragement. Finally, a very special thanks to my husband, Ross. Without his professional and emotional support, this book would still be just a dream.

Table of Contents

Creative Cards

Creative Cards

Creative Cards was developed to offer you—the busy classroom teacher—a wide variety of activities that are easy to use, easy to integrate into your regular curriculum, and fun and rewarding for your students.

As an instructor, you may ask yourself: Why should I use these picture-driven activities in my classroom? The answer is as simple as one, two, three! All activities

1. Require minimal preparation;

2. Provide an exciting stimulus for meaningful language production;

3. Are exciting and inspirational.

In addition, all activities are easy to understand, and all the pictures you need are included and ready for immediate use. All picture cards are a comfortable size, and lost or damaged cards can be quickly replaced. Finally, you can copy as many cards as needed for any given activity, thus assuring that students participate fully.

In short, using the activities in *Creative Cards* means less work for you and more enjoyment for your students.

PICTURES AND LANGUAGE LEARNING

Finding practical and successful ways to help your students enjoy language learning is often difficult. Many classroom teachers have discovered that pictures are useful aids in achieving this goal. By stimulating curiosity and interest, pictures can greatly contribute to language learning. They give students a specific point to talk or write about, or they act as a reference for further discussion.

In addition to stimulating thought and language, pictures are also useful in helping to build context. Most language is, of course, defined by the context in which it occurs. Pictures can represent and contribute

Introduction

much to the creation of context to give students a familiar, albeit nonverbal, reference point from which to proceed. Pictures also help to introduce cultural context. As language and culture are so closely connected, this contribution to language learning is indeed necessary.

The flexibility of pictures is also beneficial. In most classrooms, pictures can be used for a variety of purposes such as teaching grammar, vocabulary, conversation, listening comprehension, and reading and writing.

ORGANIZATION AND DEFINITION OF TERMS

Part I of *Creative Cards* contains 60 suggested activities for using pictures in the language classroom. One or two variations are also presented with each activity. The activities are divided into four broad categories:

1. Vocabulary practice

2. Grammar practice

3. Story creation

4. Free conversation.

While all activities can be used to practice several different aspects of the language, each has been designed to focus on one of these four areas.

All activities are presented in a similar way. At the top of each activity page is an information box. This information box can help you quickly decide if a certain activity is appropriate for your particular group and situation.

Introduction

Look, for example, at the following information:

Activity type: Story creation

Time: 20 minutes

Number of players: Small groups

Materials: Five different object cards for each group

The focus of this particular activity is on creating a story. The activity lasts approximately 20 minutes, is meant for small group work, and requires object cards.

The terms in the information section are defined as follows:

Activity Type: Which of the four general categories—vocabulary, grammar, story creation, or free conversation—the activity falls under.

Time: The approximate amount of time necessary for this activity. (This does not include preparation time.)

Number of players: The number of players needed for an activity. Class refers to large group work, small groups to groups of three or four, pairs and individual are self-explanatory.

Materials: The kind and number of cards needed for the activity. There are two types of pictures included in *Creative Cards*. Object cards are pictures of individual nouns, whereas scene cards are more complex and detailed images.

Following the information section, the procedure for each activity is described in detail. In most cases, one or two variations of the activity are also suggested. The variations are usually more challenging, as they require more from your students and less from you.

Part II of *Creative Cards* contains 50 pages of ready-to-use picture cards. As previously mentioned, there are two types of cards: object cards and scene cards. Both types of cards act as stimuli for language production. The cards have been arranged according to twelve themes: animals, clothing, environment, food, health, holidays, occupations, people, school, sports, technology, and transportation and travel. All activities can be done using any one or a mixture of these themes; the thematic focus is up to you.

Part III of *Creative Cards* includes six appendices and a brief bibliography. Appendices one through four offer easy reference guides to the activities. Respectively, they allow you to locate a specific activity according to activity type, object or scene card use, number of players, or language skill area. The final two appendices are a listing of all pictures by theme, and a template for creating your own set of cards.

Creative Cards

TIPS FOR USE

recommend utilizing the activities in this book in one of four ways. First, try using them as a warm-up: at the beginning of class, ease your students into another day of language learning. Second, try any of these activities as a way to review vocabulary or grammar structures. Most students will enjoy the games, and it gives you a new way to present the material. Third, you can use any of these activities as a time-filler-those last fifteen minutes of class, for instance, when it is too late to begin a new unit. Finally, use any of these exercises to keep your students excited about learning new language. When a particular lesson is difficult or the students seem to be having trouble concentrating, simply insert a quick picture-card activity. In most cases this will help students relax and refocus on the task at hand.

COMMENTS

All activities in *Creative Cards* were designed with the pictures in Part II in mind. Therefore, it is not necessary to spend extra preparation time searching for appropriate pictures. However, any additional pictures you come across or already have in a picture file will work as well and will add variety.

While all activities in this book have proven to be successful, they are by no means the only ways to use the enclosed picture cards. In fact, I hope that the suggested activities will act as a creative stimulus so that you can adapt and invent new activities appropriate for your particular students. The vast majority of activities in *Creative Cards* have been developed and adapted over many years of working in an ESL class-room. To create activities that met the ever-changing needs of my students, it was necessary to draw from several methods and approaches. Where activities were adapted from other sources, the original source has been cited.

HAVE FUN!

The Author

Creative Cards

Activity type: Grammar practice

Time: 10-15 minutes

Number of players: Pairs

Materials: A copy of the same object card
for each pair

PROCEDURE

1. Divide the class into pairs.

2. Give one partner from each pair a copy of the same object card.

3. Ask each partner to do the following:

   - NOT show the picture to his/her partner.

   - Describe the picture in detail for his/her partner.

4. Ask the other partner to do the following:

   - Listen carefully to the description.

   - Draw the picture that is being described in as much detail as possible.

5. Ask each pair to compare its drawing with the object cards.

6. Display all the drawings. Which pair produced the most accurate one?

VARIATION 1

- Use one object card.

- Describe it for the class as a whole.

- Ask each student to listen to your directions and try to recreate the picture.

- Display the finished products and see who reproduced the most accurate picture.

VARIATION 2

- Give each pair a different object card.

- Ask each pair to do the following:

   - Write a set of step-by-step instructions for reproducing the drawing.

   - Exchange instructions with another pair.

   - Read the new set of instructions and try to recreate the described picture.

   - Compare each drawing with the original object card.

Today or Yesterday?

Activity type: Grammar practice

Time: Varies greatly according to the level of the students

Number of players: Individuals/pairs

Materials: One scene card for each student

PROCEDURE

1. Give each student a different scene card.

2. Ask each student to do the following:

   - Write one sentence in the present continuous tense describing the scene.

   - Exchange papers with a partner.

   - Rewrite the new sentence in the simple past tense.

   Example: The man is cooking lunch.–The man cooked lunch yesterday.

3. To extend this activity, ask students to repeat it with different cards.

VARIATION 1

- Give each student a different scene card.

- Ask each student to do the following:

  - Look at his/her card and create a short story. (Six or seven sentences is a good length.)

  - Write the story in the present tense.

  - Exchange stories with a partner.

  - Rewrite the new story in the simple past tense.

VARIATION 2

- Repeat Variation 1.

- Choose more tenses and more complex tenses.

Creative Cards

Activity type: Grammar practice

Time: 10-15 minutes

Number of Players: Class

Materials: One object card for each student

PROCEDURE

1. Ask students to randomly choose five to ten object cards from your working file.

2. Without looking, mix them up and put them face down on the table in a pile.

3. Choose the top card, but do not look at it.

4. Hold the card so that the class can see it but you cannot.

5. Try to discover what you "are" by asking the class yes/no questions.

6. The students may respond only with *yes* or *no*.

7. When you have guessed correctly, repeat the steps with the next card.

8. Continue until all the cards have been used.

VARIATION 1

- Give each student a different object card.

- For increased difficulty, choose cards from several different and unrelated themes.

- Tape one card to each student's back.

- Each student must discover what he/she "is."

- The students may not look at their own cards.

- They must ask their classmates questions.

- Only yes/no questions are allowed.

- When a student guesses correctly, he/she may sit down.

- Continue until all students are seated.

What's Happening?

Activity type: Grammar practice

Time: 10-15 minutes

Number of players: Pairs

Materials: One scene card for each pair

PROCEDURE

1. Divide the class into pairs.

2. Give each pair a different scene card.

3. Ask each pair to do the following:

   - Study the card for one minute.

   - Consider the question: What's happening in my picture?

   - Talk about what's happening in the picture.

VARIATION 1

- Repeat steps 1 through 3.

- Speculate on WHY it's happening and what the consequences, if any, will be.

VARIATION 2

- Give each student a different scene card.

- Ask each student to do the following:

  - Study his/her card for two or three minutes and consider the question: What's happening in my picture?

- After a few minutes, ask all students (with their cards) to stand and gather in the middle of the room.

- Ask every student to do the following:

  - Find one partner.

  - Explain what's happening in his/her picture.

  - Listen to his/her partner's explanation.

  - Find a new partner and repeat the procedure.

- Continue for as long as desired.

Creative Cards

Activity type: Grammar practice

Time: 10-15 minutes

Number of players: Individual

Materials: One scene card for each student

PROCEDURE

1. Give each student a different scene card.

2. Choose one preposition to focus on.

3. Write your chosen preposition on the board. (Suggestions: *in, on, under, next to,* or *between*)

4. Ask each student to orally make one sentence describing his/her card.

5. He/she must use the focus preposition at least twice.

6. Continue until all students have had a turn.

VARIATION 1

- Give each student a different scene card.

- Write the following prepositions on the board: *in, on, under, next to, between.*

- Ask each student to write a short paragraph describing the card.

- He/she must use each preposition at least once.

- Ask students to share pictures and paragraphs with a partner.

VARIATION 2

- Repeat the first four steps of Variation 1.

- Collect all cards and stories.

- Display all the cards for the class.

- Mix up the stories and randomly choose one or two.

- Read the story and have the class identify the correct picture.

Hint
Use these activities to spice up your regular grammar text.

Activity Type: Grammar practice

Time: 15-20 minutes

Number of players: Small groups

Materials: Six object cards for each group

PROCEDURE

1. Divide the class into groups of four.

2. Give each group the same six object cards.

3. Ask each group to do the following:

   - Spread the cards face up on the table.

   - Sit around the table with their hands in their laps.

4. Describe one of the cards without giving the name of the object.

5. Use as many diverse adjectives as possible.

6. Instruct the students to listen and grab the correct card when they think they have correctly identified the object.

7. The first student in each group to grab the correct card gets one point.

8. If a student takes the wrong card, he/she loses one point.

9. After each round, put the card back on the table.

10. Continue until one student has five points. He/she is the winner.

VARIATION 1

- Ask the students to give the descriptions.

VARIATION 2

- Use ten to twelve cards per group.

Creative Cards

Activity type: Grammar practice

Time: 15 minutes

Number of players: Class

Materials: One enlarged scene card

PROCEDURE

1. Display one enlarged scene card for the class.

2. Assign each student a number.

3. Ask general questions about the scene, such as: Where is he?

4. Ask student number one to answer the question. (Example: He's in Canada.)

5. Ask student number two to ask a new but related question. (Example: Why did he go to Canada?)

6. Continue until all the students have asked or answered a question.

7. Use this as a review of question forms.

VARIATION 1

- Repeat steps 1 through 6.

- As a follow-up, ask each student to write a short story using the answers to the questions.

VARIATION 2

- Restrict the types of questions that the students may ask.

- Some question types include yes/no questions or WH-questions.

VARIATION 3

- Time the activity.

- Give a time limit for coming up with an appropriate question.

Photo Album

Activity type: Grammar practice

Time: 30 minutes

Number of players: Class

Materials: One scene card for each student

PROCEDURE

1. Ask the class to sit in a circle.

2. Give each student a different scene card.

3. Ask the class to imagine that each card is a photo.

4. Go around the circle and ask each student to do the following:

   - Show his/her card to the class.

   - Briefly describe what is happening in the picture.

   This is an exciting way to review the present continuous tense.

VARIATION 1

- Repeat steps 1 through 4.

- Ask each student to also tell the class what happened the day before the picture was taken.

  This is a fun way to review the simple past tense.

VARIATION 2

- Repeat steps 1 through 4.

- Ask each student to explain what happened the day before the picture was taken and what will happen tomorrow.

  This is an interesting way to review the simple past and future tenses.

Hint
Correct students' mistakes by modeling the correct form.

Creative Cards

Activity type: Grammar practice

Time: 20 minutes

Number of players: Pairs

Materials: One scene card for each pair

PROCEDURE

1. Divide the class into pairs.

2. Give each pair a different scene card.

3. Tell the class that they are newspaper reporters and that their picture is from a breaking news story.

4. Ask each pair to write a brief news story.

5. Form groups of six.

6. Share pictures and stories in the small group.

VARIATION 1

- Collect all of the stories and produce a class newspaper.

- Ask the class to choose some other items to include in the newspaper, such as a gossip column, advertisements, or comic strips.

VARIATION 2

- Give each pair three scene cards.

- Give the following directions:

  Your pictures came from the photographer of a breaking news story. The written information has been lost, and you will be on the air in ten minutes. Create a three-minute statement for the five o'clock news.

- Ask each pair to perform a short role-play.

Note: Variation 2 is based on an idea by Karin Van der Auwera of Stuttgart, Germany.

Lost and Found

Activity type: Grammar practice

Time: 15 minutes

Number of players: Pairs

Materials: Six different object cards for each pair

PROCEDURE

1. Divide the class into pairs.

2. Give each pair six different object cards.

3. Ask each pair to stack the cards face down in a pile on the table.

4. Tell the class that one partner has lost an important item and that he/she will describe it to his/her partner.

5. Ask one partner in each pair to do the following:

   - Pick the top card.

   - Identify the picture without showing it to his/her partner.

   - Describe the object in detail

     • This is big.

     • This is usually yellow.

     • This is a fruit.

6. The other partner must guess what was lost.

7. When a correct guess is made, repeat with the next card in the pile.

8. Continue until all the cards have been "found."

VARIATION 1

• Repeat steps 1 through 8.

• Limit the number of descriptive sentences allowed for each object.

VARIATION 2

• Set a time limit.

• The pair with the most "found" objects within the time limit is the winner.

Creative Cards

Activity: Grammar practice

Time: 10 minutes

Number of players: Pairs

Materials: One scene card for each pair

Is the penny under the elephant? No, it isn't.

Is the penny in the lion's mouth? Yes, it is.

PROCEDURE

1. Divide the class into pairs.

2. Give each pair one scene card.

3. Give the following directions:

   Each partner should quietly study the scene. Pretend you are going to hide a penny. Think of a good hiding place, but do not tell your partner where it is. Take turns guessing where your partner has hidden the penny. You may ask only yes/no questions, and you may answer only yes or no.

4. When both hiding places have been found, the round is over.

5. Play as many rounds as you like.

VARIATION 1

- Allow the students to give clues to their hiding place using prepositions.

  Example: It is near the_____, or it is between the_____ and the_____.

Descriptions

Activity type: Grammar practice

Time: 15 minutes

Number of players: Class

Materials: One object card per student and one blank sheet of paper per student

PROCEDURE

1. Choose one object card and display an enlarged copy for the class.

2. Using one adjective, write a simple phrase describing the object. (Example: The big cow.)

3. Ask each student to do the following:

   - Copy the sentence you have written.

   - Pass his/her paper to the person on the right.

   - Copy the sentence again and add a SECOND adjective. (Example: The big, black cow.)

4. Continue passing and adding one new adjective until each student gets his/her original paper back.

5. Share the descriptions with the group.

VARIATION 1

- Give each student a different object card and a blank sheet of paper.

- Ask each student to do the following:

  - Identify the object on his/her card.

  - Write one sentence describing the object using one adjective of his/her choice.

  - Pass the card and paper to the person sitting to his/her right.

  - Look at the new card and read the sentence.

  - Write a second sentence, adding one new adjective.

- Repeat steps 4 and 5.

VARIATION 2

- Follow the procedures for Variation 1.

- After each student has his/her original paper back, collect all the picture cards.

- Mix up and spread out the pictures on a table.

- As each student reads his/her description, ask the other members of the class to pick out the card being described.

Creative Cards

Activity type: Grammar practice

Time: 20-25 minutes

Number of players: Small groups

Materials: One scene card for each group of four

PROCEDURE

1. Divide the class into groups of four.

2. Ask each group to appoint one student to be its "fortune-teller."

3. Give each fortune-teller one scene card.

4. Ask group members to ask their fortune-teller what the future holds.

5. The fortune-teller must use the scene card and the future tense to "tell the future."

VARIATION 1

- Repeat steps 1 through 5, EXCEPT give each fortune-teller three scene cards.

- Ask the fortune-teller to choose which fortune to give to the group.

VARIATION 2

- Give each group one scene card.

- Ask them to discuss what is happening in the picture.

- Ask them to discuss what will happen to the people in the picture next year.

- Ask them to choose one student to act as a recorder.

- Write a one-paragraph description of the future.

- Share the stories with the class.

Note: This activity is based on an idea by Karin Van der Auwera of Stuttgart, Germany.

Comparisons

Activity type: Grammar practice

Time: 10-15 minutes

Number of players: Small groups

Materials: Two different scene cards for each group

PROCEDURE

1. Divide the class into groups of three.

2. Give each group two different scene cards.

3. Ask each group to examine the two cards, noting any similarities.

4. Ask each group to share its findings with the class.

VARIATION 1

• Display two enlarged scene cards for the class.

• Working as a class, list five similarities between the two cards.

• In more advanced classes, ask students to focus on broader similarities.

VARIATION 2

• Do this activity as a competition.

• The group with the largest number of similarities is the winner.

VARIATION 3

• Note both similarities and differences.

Creative Cards

Activity type: Grammar practice

Time: 25-30 minutes

Number of players: Pairs/class

Materials: A different object card for each pair

PROCEDURE

1. Divide the class into pairs.

2. Give each pair a different object card.

3. Ask each pair to write two or three sentences describing the object in a positive light.

4. Ask each pair to display its card and sentences for the rest of the class.

5. Go quickly around the room and look at each object and read the description.

6. Explain that you will now hold an auction to sell the various objects.

7. Give each pair a $50 credit, which they may use to buy the object(s) of their choice.

8. Hold the auction, selling each object to the highest bidder.

VARIATION 1

- Repeat the activity, EXCEPT do not display the pictures for the class.

- Conduct the auction based only on the written descriptions.

VARIATION 2

- Make the object of the auction to buy as many objects as possible with the $50.

- The winning pair is the one that has purchased the largest number of objects.

Spring Break

Activity Type: Grammar practice

Time: 20-30 minutes

Number of players: Pairs

Materials: Three object cards for each pair

PROCEDURE

1. Divide the class into pairs.

2. Give each pair three object cards.

3. Ask each pair to identify and write down the names of each object on a piece of paper.

4. Tell the class that they all took a vacation last spring and the objects were found in their suitcases.

5. Ask each pair to write a short description of their trip, including where they went, how long they stayed, what they did, and why they brought each of the objects on the cards.

6. Ask for volunteers to share their work with the class.

VARIATION 1

- Do the same activity, but give each pair five to seven object cards.

VARIATION 2

- Ask each pair to create a travel brochure to lure other vacationers to their destination.

- Ask the class to vote on a destination for a class field trip.

Creative Cards

Activity type: Story creation

Time: 25 minutes

Number of players: Class

Materials: One or two enlarged scene cards

PROCEDURE

1. Choose, enlarge, and display any one scene card.

2. Write a one- or two-sentence story beginning on the board. Read it as a class.

3. Ask each student to do the following:

   - Copy the beginning on a separate sheet of paper.

   - Add one to three sentences to continue the story.

   - Pass his/her paper one seat to the right.

   - Add one to three new sentences to the story in front of him/her.

4. Continue until each student has his/her original paper back.

5. Share the stories with the class or in small groups.

VARIATION 1

- Repeat step 1.

- As a class create a one- or two-sentence story using the card as a cue.

- Repeat steps 3 through 5.

VARIATION 2

- Choose and enlarge any two scene cards.

- Divide the class into two groups.

- Give one card to group one and the other card to group two.

- Don't let either group see the other group's card.

- Ask each group to do the following:

  - Create and write a story beginning using its card on one sheet of paper.

  - Exchange papers but NOT CARDS with the other group.

  - Work together to finish the other group's story without looking at the card.

- When both groups are finished, display both cards and share the stories.

- Compare the scenes with the stories—are they related?

Experiences

Activity type: Story creation

Time: 15-20 minutes

Number of players: Small groups/class

Materials: The same scene card for each group of five

PROCEDURE

1. Make an enlarged copy of one scene card and display it for the class.

2. As a class, brainstorm words and expressions associated with the picture.

3. Record the students' ideas on the board.

4. Ask: "Have you ever been in the same situation as the person/people in the picture? What happened?"

5. Ask individuals to share their experiences with the class.

VARIATION 1

- Divide the class into groups of five.

- Give each group a copy of the SAME scene card.

- Ask each group to do the following:

  - Spend five minutes individually brainstorming personal experiences that the card evokes.

  - Share individual experiences within the small group.

  - Choose one experience from the group to share with the class.

VARIATION 2

- Repeat Variation 1.

- As a class, discuss the reasons for similar and dissimilar experiences. Do cultural, gender, socio-economic or other factors affect our experiences?

OPTION

- Ask each student to do a formal writing assignment based on his/her chosen experience.

Creative Cards

Activity type: Story creation

Time: 30-45 minutes

Number of players: Small groups

Materials: Five object cards for each group of four

PROCEDURE

1. Give each group the same five object cards.

2. Ask each group to create a short story and to select a spokesperson to share it with the class.

3. Share stories.

4. Compare similarities and differences among the different groups' stories.

Hint

Creating stories can be either an oral or a written activity.

VARIATION 1

- Choose a different theme for each group.

- Give each group the same five object cards from the selected theme.

- Ask each group to create a story and to select a spokesperson to share it with the class.

- Share stories.

VARIATION 2

- Number the class off by fours.

- All the 1s are group one, all the 2s group two, all the 3s group three, and all the 4s group four.

- Assign a different theme to each group.

- Give each group a set of five object cards from its assigned theme.

- Ask each group to do the following:

  - Appoint a recorder to write the story as the group creates it.

  - Make enough copies of the finished story so that each member of the group has his/her own copy.

- Form NEW groups. Each group will now have one #1, one #2, one #3, and one #4.

- There will be four different stories in each group. Ask the students to share stories.

Creative Cards

Activity type: Story creation

Time: 15 minutes

Number of players: Pairs

Materials: One scene card for each pair
(Copy the same scene for each pair)

PROCEDURE

1. Choose a scene card that shows ONE person doing an activity.

2. Copy the card so that you have one copy for each pair of students.

3. Write the following questions on the board:

   - What is his/her name?

   - How old is he/she?

   - Is he/she married?

   - What are his/her hobbies?

4. Ask each pair to do the following:

   - Answer the questions on the board on a separate sheet of paper.

   - Use the answers to the questions to write a short story about the person on their card.

   - Share their story with one other pair.

VARIATION 1

- Choose one scene card that shows one person doing an activity.

- Enlarge the card and display it for the class.

- Repeat steps 3 and 4, EXCEPT answer the questions and create one story as a class.

- Write the story on the board.

- Ask each student to copy it into his/her notebook for additional writing practice.

Creative Cards

Activity type: Story creation

Time: 15-20 minutes (depending on the size of the class)

Number of players: Class

Materials: One different object card for each student and a story prepared before class

PROCEDURE

1. Before class:

   - Choose one different object card for each class member.

   - From these pictures create a story to tell the class.

   - Vary the complexity of the story according to the level of the class.

2. Randomly give each student an object card.

3. Tell your story to the class.

4. Ask students to listen to the story.

5. Ask students to put the pictures in the correct order.

6. Using the pictures as cues, have a volunteer retell the story.

VARIATION 1

- Divide the class into groups of four.

- Give each group a different set of four object cards.

- Ask each group to do the following:

  - Write one short story, incorporating the information on the four cards.

  - Join with a second group of four.

  - Read their story aloud, asking the other group to listen and to put the pictures in the correct order.

  - Listen to the other group's story and order their four cards correctly.

  - Choose one spokesperson to tell the OTHER GROUP'S story to the class.

VARIATION 2

- For more variety, use a mixture of scene and object cards.

Creative Cards

Activity type: Story creation

Time: 20-30 minutes

Number of players: Pairs

Materials: Five object cards for each pair

PROCEDURE

1. Divide the class into pairs.

2. Give each pair the same five object cards.

3. Read the situation.

4. Ask each pair to do the following:

   - Identify the five objects.

   - Answer the following questions based on these objects.

- How old is the man?

- What is his job?

- What are his hobbies?

5. Share ideas with the class.

Situation

Last week a new man moved in next door to you. You are very curious about him, but you have not yet met him. You decide to snoop around, so you look through his trash. The five objects you have are what you found in his garbage can.

Note: You may want to point out that snooping around in someone's trash is not a recommended activity.

VARIATION 1

- Enlarge and display five object cards.

- Identify all the objects as a class.

- Read the situation and have the class answer the three questions.

VARIATION 2

- Repeat steps 1 through 5.

- Ask students to write a paragraph about the man's life.

Creative Cards

Activity type: Story creation

Time: 30 minutes

Number of players: Small groups

Materials: One scene card for each group

PROCEDURE

1. Divide the class into groups of four.

2. Give each group one scene card.

3. Ask each group to prepare a role-play demonstrating what is on their card.

4. Ask each group to perform the role-play for the class.

VARIATION 1

- Repeat steps 1 through 4.

- After each performance, ask the rest of the class to guess what scene was on the performing group's card.

VARIATION 2

- For more advanced students, give each small group three scene cards.

- Ask each group to prepare a role-play connecting the scenes on three scene cards.

- Ask each group to perform the role-play.

- Ask the class to try to guess the content of the three cards.

Once Upon A Time

Activity type: Story creation

Time: 20-30 minutes

Number of players: Small groups

Materials: Eight to fifteen object cards per group
(Each group should have the same cards)

PROCEDURE

1. Divide the class into groups of four.

2. Give each group the same eight object cards.

3. Ask each group to do the following:

   - Choose four of the eight cards.

   - Work together to create one story.

   - Use all the chosen cards at least once.

   - Choose a recorder to write the story down.

   - Choose one spokesperson to share the story
     with the larger group.

4. Share the stories.

VARIATION 1

- Divide the class into groups of four.

- Give each group ten to fifteen object cards.

- Repeat steps 3 and 4.

VARIATION 2

- Repeat steps 1 through 4, EXCEPT give each group
  fifteen object cards.

- Tell students that ALL cards must be used at least
  once.

Hint

*In multicultural classes, encourage students to
share stories, myths, legends, and so on from
their own cultures.*

Creative Cards

Activity type: Story creation

Time: 20-25 minutes

Number of players: Small groups/class

Materials: One to three scene cards

PROCEDURE

1. Before class:

   - Choose one scene card and write a short paragraph about the picture.

   - Copy the paragraph onto index cards. Write one sentence per card.

2. Display the scene card for the class to see.

3. Divide the class into small groups.

4. Give each group one index card.

5. Ask each group to do the following:

   - Read the sentence on their index card.

   - Work with the other groups to put the sentences in the correct order.

6. Read the paragraph as a class.

7. Ask each student to copy the paragraph into his/her notebook.

VARIATION 1

- Display one enlarged scene card.

- Divide the class into groups of three.

- Ask each small group to write a short paragraph about the picture.

- Ask each group to write the paragraph on index cards—one sentence per card.

- Collect and redistribute the paragraphs.

- Reconstruct each paragraph and share with the class.

VARIATION 2

- Display three scene cards.

- Before class prepare three paragraphs, putting each sentence on one index card.

- Mix up all the index cards.

- Ask the class to work together to separate and to order the index card sentences.

- Ask the class to discuss which paragraph goes with which picture.

Sketch

Creative Cards

Activity type: Story creation

Time: 20 minutes

Number of players: Small groups

Materials: The same object card for each group

PROCEDURE

1. Divide the class into groups of three.

2. Give each group a copy of the same object card.

3. Ask the class to imagine that this picture represents the beginning of a story.

4. Ask each group to do the following:

   - Orally create the rest of the story.

   - Draw three to four additional pictures to tell the rest of the story.

   - Present the group's work to the class.

VARIATION 1

- Repeat steps 1 through 4.

- Following the presentations, ask each group to do the following:

   - Exchange pictures with another group.

   - Write out the story told by the pictures.

VARIATION 2

- Divide the class into pairs.

- Display one object card for the class to study.

- Ask each pair to do the following:

   - Draw one picture to continue the story.

   - Pass their paper to the right.

   - Add a second picture to continue the story.

   - Continue until each pair receives its original sheet.

   - Orally share the story with the rest of the class.

OPTION

- Write out the complete story.

Creative Cards

Activity type: Story creation

Time: 30 minutes

Number of players: Pairs/class

Materials: One different scene card for each pair

PROCEDURE

1. Give each pair a different card.

2. Ask each pair to write two to three sentences on a separate sheet describing the card.

3. Collect all papers and cards. Mix them up.

4. Redistribute the sentences.

5. Lay all cards out on the table.

6. Ask each pair to do the following:

   - Work together and quietly read their new sentences.

   - Match the sentences with the correct picture card.

VARIATION 1

- Repeat step 1.

- Ask each pair to create and write a one-paragraph story about the card.

- Repeat steps 3 through 6.

- Ask each pair to tell the class WHY they chose the card they did.

   (More advanced students should be quite specific and explain in detail.)

Hint

View these story times as an opportunity for students to express their thoughts and ideas in English. You may note certain grammatical problems, but don't correct at this time—simply make note of them for a later lesson. Allow students a chance at free expression and enjoy their creativity.

Creative Cards

Activity Type: Story Creation

Time: 30 minutes

Number of players: Pairs

Materials: One to five scene cards for each pair

PROCEDURE

1. Choose one theme for the class to focus on.

2. Give each pair a different scene card from the chosen theme.

3. Ask each pair to work together to create a three- or four-sentence story.

4. Orally share stories with one other pair of students.

VARIATION 1

• Choose a different theme for each pair.

• Give each pair any three scene cards from the chosen theme.

• Ask each pair to work together to write a four- or five-sentence story connecting the activities on the cards.

• Orally share the stories with the larger group.

VARIATION 2

• Repeat the first two steps of Variation 1.

• Ask each pair to do the following:

  - Work together and write a five- to ten-sentence story connecting the activities on the cards.

  - Exchange stories and pictures with another pair.

  - Look at the pictures and write three additional sentences to continue the story.

  - Share the stories with the class.

Hint
Encourage students to be creative and innovative. Anything goes!

Creative Cards

Activity type: Story creation

Time: 20 minutes (depending on the class size)

Number of players: Class

Materials: One object card for each student

PROCEDURE

1. Ask the class to sit in a circle.

2. Give each student a different object card.

3. Begin by telling a short and simple story about a man who went on vacation.

4. Choose one student to show his/her card.

5. Ask that student to identify the object on his/her card and then explain what the man did with it while on vacation.

6. Move clockwise around the circle.

7. Ask each student to show his/her card and tell what the man did with the object on vacation.

8. As the students speak, write their responses on the board.

9. After all students have spoken, reread the whole story as a class.

10. For additional practice, each student can copy the story into his/her notebook.

VARIATION 1

- Repeat steps 1 through 7.

- After all students have spoken, ask a volunteer to retell the story from memory.

VARIATION 2

- Repeat steps 1 through 7.

- When finished, ask each student to write as much of the story as he/she remembers.

- Divide the class into small groups.

- Ask students to share their stories to check for accuracy.

Switcheroo

Activity type: Story creation

Time: 25-30 minutes (depending on class size)

Number of players: Class/pairs

Materials: One enlarged scene card

PROCEDURE

1. Display one enlarged scene card for the class.

2. As a group, create a short story about the picture.

3. Write the story on the board for reference.

4. Choose one **noun** in the picture, circle it, and change it to something else.

   How does this affect the story?

   The woman is now a lion.

5. Ask each student to rewrite the story, taking into account the change.

6. Share stories with the class.

VARIATION 1

- Divide the class into pairs.

- Give each pair a different scene card.

- Ask each pair to do the following:

  - Write a story about their card.

  - Decide which noun to change.

  - Pass the story card and change to a neighboring pair.

  - Rewrite the new story, incorporating the change.

  - Share stories with the class.

Creative Cards

Activity type: Story creation

Time: 15-25 minutes (depending on the size of the class)

Number of players: Class

Materials: One different object card for each student

PROCEDURE

1. Ask the students to sit in a circle.

2. Give each student a different object card.

3. Choose one student to show his/her card.

4. Ask that student to begin a story with two or three sentences incorporating his/her object.

5. Move clockwise around the circle.

6. Ask each student to show his/her card and orally continue the story.

7. As students speak, write their sentences on the board.

8. After all students have spoken, reread the story as a class.

9. For additional practice, each student can copy the story into his/her notebook.

VARIATION 1

- Repeat steps 1 through 6.

- After all the students have spoken, choose one to retell the complete story for the class.

- To add variety, use a mixture of scene and object cards.

VARIATION 2

- Repeat steps 1 through 6.

- When finished, ask each student to write as much of the story as he/she remembers.

- Divide the class into small groups and ask them to share stories and check for accuracy.

Creative Cards

Activity type: Vocabulary practice

Time: 10-15 minutes

Number of players: Class

Materials: One different object card per round

PROCEDURE

1. Ask the class to sit in a circle.

2. Give one volunteer one object card.

3. Instruct the volunteer NOT to show the card to the other students.

4. Ask the volunteer to whisper the name of the object to the student on his/her right.

5. Ask this second student to whisper the word he/she heard to the student on his/her right.

6. Continue until the word has been whispered all around the circle.

7. Ask the last student to say the word aloud.

8. Look at the card—did the student say the correct word?

9. Repeat as often as desired with different pictures.

VARIATION 1

• Begin the round yourself.

• Do not give the name of the object.

• Identify what is on the card, but whisper, "This is used for _____."

• The last student says the sentence, and the class has to guess what object is on the card.

• For more advanced groups, ask a student to begin each round.

VARIATION 2

• Repeat Variation 1, EXCEPT use adjectives to describe the object.

    Example: "This is round, sour, and yellow. What is it?"

Creative Cards

Activity type: Vocabulary practice

Time: 20 minutes

Number of players: Class

Materials: One object card for each student

PROCEDURE

1. Before class:

   - Choose one object card for each student.

   - Write a one- or two-sentence riddle about each picture.

   Example: I am big and have a long nose.

2. Display all the object cards for the class to see.

3. Distribute one riddle per student.

4. Ask each student to do the following:

   - Read his/her riddle.

   - Choose the matching object card.

5. Check as a class.

VARIATION 1

- Display five object cards for the class.

- Divide the class into groups of four.

- Ask each group to secretly choose one picture and write (as a group) a riddle.

- Ask each group to read their riddle.

- Ask the class to guess which is the corresponding picture.

VARIATION 2

- Give each pair of students one object card.

- Ask each pair to write a one-sentence riddle.

- Collect all the cards and spread them out face up on one table.

- Collect all riddles, mix them up, and redistribute them.

- Ask each pair to match their riddle with the correct picture.

Creative Cards

Activity type: Vocabulary practice

Time: 10 minutes

Number of players: Class

Materials: One enlarged scene card

PROCEDURE

1. Display one enlarged scene card for the class.

2. Ask the class to silently study the picture for 30 seconds.

3. Do not allow them to write anything down during these 30 seconds.

4. After the time is up, cover the picture.

5. Ask each student to write down as many details as he/she can remember.

6. Uncover the picture and ask the students to check their work.

VARIATION 1

- Divide the class into two groups.

- Show each group a different scene card for 45 seconds.

- Ask students to write as many details as they remember from the picture they saw.

- Ask each student in group one to exchange his/her paper with a student from group two.

- Ask each student to read the list of details he/she has just received.

- Can the students in group one recreate (draw) the picture from group two?

- Can the students in group two recreate (draw) the picture from group one?

- Compare each group's drawing with the original picture.

Note: This activity is based on the activity Street Scene found in *The Interactive Tutorial* by Karen Sanders.

Creative Cards

Activity type: Vocabulary practice

Time: 20 minutes

Number of players: Pairs

Materials: Six blank cards for each pair and the same six object cards for each pair

PROCEDURE

1. Choose any theme.

2. Give each pair the same six object cards.

3. As a group, identify the six objects.

4. Give each pair six blank cards.

5. Ask each pair to do the following:

   - Write the names of the objects on the blank cards (one name per card).

   - Turn all 12 cards face down and mix them up.

   - Arrange the 12 cards in three rows of four.

   - Choose one partner to turn over two cards.

6. If it is a match (picture and name) the student keeps the two cards and takes another turn.

7. If there is no match, the turn is over and the student should return the cards face down to their original positions.

8. It is now the other student's turn.

9. Continue until all the matching pairs have been found.

10. Use this game as a vocabulary review activity.

Hint

For more advanced students, encourage the use of an English-English dictionary whenever possible.

Matisse Magic

Activity type: Vocabulary practice

Time: 20 minutes

Number of players: Individual

Materials: A different object card for each student

PROCEDURE

1. Give each student a different object card.

2. Ask each student to do the following:

   - Identify his/her object for the class.

   - Glue or tape his/her picture on a larger sheet of paper.

   - Draw in a scene around the object, incorporating it into a larger picture.

   - Exchange finished drawings with a neighbor.

   - Label, with the correct words, ten items on the recently acquired picture.

   - Present this vocabulary to the class.

VARIATION 1

- Divide the class into pairs.

- Give each pair three different object cards.

- Ask each pair to draw a scene incorporating all three objects.

- Repeat step 2.

VARIATION 2

- For beginning-level classes, give each student the same card and allow them to work in groups.

Creative Cards

Activity type: Vocabulary practice

Time: 15-25 minutes

Number of players: Small groups

Materials: 12 object cards for each group

PROCEDURE

1. Divide the class into groups of three or four.

2. On the board write the following sentence:

A. What can you do with a _____?

3. Give each group 12 object cards.

4. Ask each group to do the following:

- Pile their cards face down on the table.

- Turn over the top card and identify the object.

- Read the sentence and fill in the blank with the name of the object.

Example: What can you do with a taco?

- Discuss possible answers to Question A.

- After two to three minutes, repeat with the next card.

5. Continue for as long as desired or until all the cards have been discussed.

Note: This activity is based on an idea by Jo Sanders.

VARIATION 1

- Repeat steps 1 and 2.

- Write the following sentence on the board:

   B. What can you do with a _____ AND a_____ ?

- Repeat steps 3 and 4, EXCEPT:

   - Ask them to turn over two cards at a time.

   - Discuss possible answers to Question B.

VARIATION 2

- Write the following sentence on the board:

C. Why does the _____ have a _____ in his/her pocket?

- Give each group any ten blank cards AND ten object cards.

- Ask each group to do the following:

   - Brainstorm ten "people" vocabulary words: woman, doctor, girl, and so on.

   - Write one word on each of the ten blank cards.

   - Make two piles on the table: pile 1 = word cards, and pile 2 = picture cards.

- Repeat steps 3 and 4, EXCEPT:

   - Turn over one card from each pile.

   - Discuss possible answers to Question C.

I Can!

Activity type: Vocabulary practice

Time: 20 minutes

Number of players: Pairs

Materials: One different object card for each pair

PROCEDURE

1. Divide the class into pairs.

2. Give each pair a different object card.

3. Write the following phrase on the board: With this object I can _____ .

4. Ask each pair to brainstorm things that they can do with the object on their card.

5. Ask each pair to complete the phrase on the board four times.

6. Set a two-minute time limit.

7. After two minutes, ask each pair to exchange cards with a neighboring pair.

8. Spend two more minutes brainstorming uses for the second object.

9. Ask neighboring pairs to form groups of four.

10. Share ideas and sentences with the class.

VARIATION 1

- Display one enlarged object card for the class.

- Divide the class into pairs.

- Repeat steps 3 through 6.

- Ask each pair to share one idea with the larger group.

VARIATION 2

- At the conclusion of the activity, ask each student to choose one of the ideas and expand on it.

- This expansion activity can be either written (ask them to write a complete paragraph) or oral (ask them to explain their ideas in more detail to their partners).

Creative Cards

Activity type: Vocabulary practice

Time: 15-20 minutes

Number of players: Class

Materials: One different object card for each student

PROCEDURE

1. Ask the class to sit in a circle.

2. Give each student a different object card.

3. On the board write: For my birthday I got a _____.

4. Ask one student to show his/her card to the class and read the sentence, completing it with the name of the object on his/her card.

5. Ask the next student to show his/her card, and complete the sentence with the name of the object on his/her card.

6. Continue around the circle until all students have had a turn.

VARIATION 1

• Write the following sentence on the board: For my birthday I wanted a _____, but I got a _____.

• Ask each student to do the following:

  - Fill in the first blank with the object on his/her card.

  - Pick a classmate's object to fill in the second blank.

• Continue around the circle until all students have had a turn.

VARIATION 2

• Ask students to do Variation 1, BUT ask them to turn their cards face down before beginning.

Countdown

Activity type: Vocabulary practice

Time: 15-20 minutes

Number of players: Pairs

Materials: Two object cards and one sheet of blank paper for each student

PROCEDURE

1. Give each student two object cards and a blank sheet of paper.

2. Check that each student knows the names of his/her objects and how to spell each one.

3. Ask each student to put in the correct number of blanks for each word.

4. Ask each student to write the numbers one to ten under the blanks.

5. Divide the class into pairs.

6. Read the rules as a class.

7. Review all vocabulary as a group at the conclusion of the game.

RULES

- Try to guess your partner's word.

- You may guess one letter at a time.

- If you guess a letter that is in the word, your partner will put it in the correct blank.

- If you make an incorrect guess, your partner will cross out one number.

- If the "countdown" is completed before you guess the word, your partner wins.

- If you guess the word before your partner reaches 0, you win.

School bus

Taco

X̶X̶X̶X̶X̶X̶6 5 4 3 2 1 0   X̶X̶X̶X̶X̶X̶X̶X̶3 2 1 0

S _ _ o o _   T a c o

_ _ s

Note: This activity is based on the popular word game "Hangman."

Creative Cards

Activity type: Vocabulary practice

Time: Varies

Number of players: Class

Materials: A different object card for each student

PROCEDURE

1. Choose a theme that the class has been working on.

2. Give each student an object card from that theme.

3. Ask the class to stand and gather in the middle of the room.

4. Ask each student to find a partner.

5. Each partner identifies the object on his/her card.

6. After each student has spoken, they should EXCHANGE cards and find a new partner.

7. Students can work at their own pace and change partners as often as they like.

VARIATION 1

- Repeat steps 1 through 4.

- Step 5: Ask each partner to identify the object on his/her card AND describe its function.

- Repeat steps 6 and 7.

VARIATION 2

- Repeat steps 1 through 7.

- After five minutes, ask the students to return to their seats.

- Ask each student to write down all the objects he/she remembers seeing.

- The student with the most correct objects wins a prize.

Note: This activity is based on an idea presented by Kathy Diaz at the 1995 TESOL conference In Long Beach, Calif.

Building Blocks

Creative Cards

Activity type: Vocabulary practice

Time: 10-15 minutes

Number of players: Class

Materials: One object card for each student

PROCEDURE:

1. Ask the class to sit in a circle.

2. Ask each student to hold his/her card so that all cards are visible to the whole class.

3. Begin by saying (for example), "I have a cow."

4. Ask the student to your right to continue by saying, "I have a banana; she has a cow."

5. Ask the next student to continue, "I have a truck; she has a banana; she has a cow."

6. Continue counterclockwise around the circle until all the students have had a turn.

7. The final student will have to name all of the objects.

8. Conclude the activity by asking the class to repeat as you quickly name all of the objects.

VARIATION 1

- After going around one time to familiarize the students with the vocabulary, do a SPEED round.

VARIATION 2

- Repeat steps 1 through 6 two or three times.

- Ask all the students to turn their cards face down.

- Try to name all the objects from memory.

Creative Cards

Activity Type: Vocabulary Practice

Time: 15-20 minutes

Number of players: Pairs

Materials: 12 object cards for each pair

PROCEDURE

1. Give each pair twelve object cards from ONE chosen theme.

2. Ask each pair to do the following:

   - Stack the cards face down in one pile on the table.

   - Turn over the top card.

   - Identify the item on the card.

   - Write down the identified vocabulary on a separate sheet of paper.

   - Turn over the next card in the pile and repeat the task, continuing the vocabulary list.

   - Continue until all the cards have been identified.

   This activity will help students create their own vocabulary study guides.

VARIATION 1

- Repeat steps 1 and 2.

- Brainstorm and add ten related words to the list.

Hint

Ask students to maintain a "vocabulary journal" throughout the class. Every time they come across a new word, in or out of class, they should record it in their journal.

Vocabulary List

Activity type: Vocabulary practice

Time: 15-20 minutes

Number of players: Individuals/small groups

Materials: One scene card for each student/group

PROCEDURE

1. Choose one theme.

2. Divide the class into groups of three.

3. Give each group a different scene card from that theme. If necessary, some groups may have duplicate cards.

4. Ask each group to do the following:

   - Study the scene.

   - Work together to make one list of all recognized vocabulary.

5. Collect each group's list and compile a comprehensive vocabulary list for that theme based on the class's work.

6. Distribute the comprehensive list to all students.

VARIATION 1

- Give each student a different scene card from one theme. If necessary, some students may have duplicate cards.

- Ask each student to do the following:

   - Study the scene.

   - Make a list of all known vocabulary.

   - Turn in the list to the teacher.

- Repeat steps 5 and 6.

VARIATION 2

- Repeat Variation 1, BUT do not ask the students to turn in their lists to you.

- After each student has developed a short list, divide the class into groups of four.

- Ask each group to compile a comprehensive list from the individual ones.

- Collect these student-generated lists and compile a master vocabulary list for that theme.

- Copy and distribute the master list to the whole class.

Creative Cards

Activity type: Free conversation

Time: 25 minutes

Number of players: Small groups

Materials: One scene card for each group of three

PROCEDURE

1. Divide the class into groups of three.

2. Give each group one scene card.

3. Ask each group to do the following:

   - Write an advertisement for this destination.

   - Show the scene card and present the advertisement to the class.

   - Try to convince the class to go to this spot for a vacation.

4. After all groups have presented, ask the class to vote on the destination for their next vacation.

VARIATION 1

- Extend this activity by planning a trip to the desired destination.

- Ask each group to make a list of what they would like to bring and what they will do there.

Twins

Creative Cards

Activity type: Free conversation

Time: 20 minutes

Number of players: Pairs

Materials: Two six-card sets for each pair
(One set = six different scene cards)

PROCEDURE

1. Divide the class into pairs.

2. Give each student his/her own set of cards.
   (See "material" note above.)

3. Ask each student to shuffle his/her set and put it in
   a pile face down on the table.

4. Ask each partner to do the following:

   - Choose the top card from the pile.

   - Describe the card to his/her partner. (Do not
     show the card.)

   - Decide, without looking, if each partner has the
     same card.

5. If each partner holds the same card, it is a match.

6. Put the matches aside and continue by drawing the
   next top card in each pile.

7. If the cards are different, return them randomly to
   the pile and continue with the next top cards.

8. Continue until all six pairs have been matched.

VARIATION 1

• Repeat steps 1 through 7, EXCEPT give each
  student very similar and/or more cards in each set.

Creative Cards

Activity type: Free conversation

Time: 10 minutes per round

Number of players: Pairs

Materials: The same object card for each pair

PROCEDURE

1. Divide the class into pairs.

2. In each pair, assign a partner A and a partner B.

3. Give each partner A a copy of the same object card.

4. Do NOT show the card to partner B.

5. Write three words on the board that are usually used to describe the object.

ball
round
throw

Example: Three off-limits words could be ball, round, and throw.

6. Partner A's task is to describe the object on the card without using the three off-limits words.

7. When partner B correctly guesses the word, the round is complete.

VARIATION 1

• Choose one student to come to the front of the room.

• Give him/her one object card.

• Write two off-limits words on the board.

• Ask the student to describe the object to the class without using the two off-limits words.

• When someone guesses correctly, repeat with a different student and a different object card.

VARIATION 2

• Repeat steps 1 through 7, EXCEPT the only word that is off limits is the name of the object.

Note: This activity is based on an idea by Karin Van der Auwera of Stuttgart, Germany.

Matchmaker

Activity type: Free conversation

Time: 10 minutes

Number of players: Class/pairs

Material: Enough scene cards for half of the class
(Example: If you have a class of twenty, you will need ten cards)

PROCEDURE

1. Before class:

   - Choose and copy enough scene cards for half the class.

   - Cut each card in half.

   - Mix up all the half-cards.

2. Give each student half a scene card.

3. Ask each student to find the classmate with the matching half of his/her card.

4. When all the matches have been found, ask each pair to answer the question: What is happening in our picture?

VARIATION 1

- Instead of mingling, ask one volunteer to describe his/her card to the class.

- Ask the rest of the students to listen and try to determine if his/her card is a match.

- After the first match has been found, repeat with a new volunteer.

VARIATION 2

- After all students have found a match, ask them to sit with their partner.

- Ask each pair to write a short story describing their picture.

Creative Cards

Activity type: Free conversation

Time: 10-15 minutes

Number of players: Class

Materials: A different scene card for each student

PROCEDURE

1. Give each student a different scene card.

2. Ask half of the class to form a circle, facing out.

3. Ask the other half to form a second circle, facing in. (See diagram.)

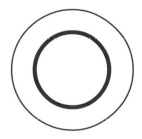

4. Ask each student to take a turn describing his/her card to the person across from him/her.

5. After two minutes, ask the outer circle to move one person to the right.

6. Ask students to talk about their cards to their new partners.

7. Continue for ten minutes or until the students are back to their original positions.

VARIATION 1

- Repeat steps 1 through 3.

- Ask each student to explain what's happening in his/her picture with the person across from him/her.

- Repeat steps 5 through 7.

VARIATION 2

- Repeat steps 1 through 3.

- Ask each student to explain what is happening in his/her picture with his/her partner.

- Ask each student to also give his/her opinion on WHY.

- Repeat steps 5 through 7.

Hint

For large classes, form two or three sets of circles.

Conversation Starters

Activity type: Free conversation

Time: 10-15 minutes

Number of players: Pairs

Materials: 10 scene cards for each pair

PROCEDURE

1. Divide the class into pairs.

2. Give each pair a stack of scene cards (about 10 cards per pair).

3. Ask one student to turn over the top card.

4. Describe the card in detail.

5. After one minute, turn over the next card.

6. Describe in detail.

7. Continue as long as desired or until all the cards have been used.

VARIATION 1

- Repeat steps 1 and 2.

- Discuss the scene. Share personal experiences related to the scene.

- After two to three minutes, turn over the next card.

- Discuss and share personal experiences.

- Continue as long as desired or until all the cards have been used.

Hint

You can extend this activity by rotating the cards among different groups. For example, when all groups are through with their cards, have them exchange stacks with the neighboring group.

Note: This activity is based on an idea presented by Kathy Diaz at the 1995 TESOL conference in Long Beach, Calif.

Creative Cards

Activity type: Free conversation

Time: 15-20 minutes

Number of players: Small groups

Materials: Six scene cards for each group of four

PROCEDURE

1. Divide the class into groups of four.

2. Give each group six scene cards.

3. Ask each group to lay the cards face up in a row on the table.

4. Ask students to take turns within their groups addressing each card.

5. Each student should talk briefly about the first card. What does it remind him/her of?

6. When each of the four have talked about the first card, they should move on to the second card.

7. Continue until each group has briefly addressed all six cards.

VARIATION 1

- Repeat steps 1 through 7.

- Ask each student to choose one card to write about.

- Ask each student to write one paragraph about his/her experiences related to the chosen card.

- Divide the class into pairs. Avoid pairing students who were in the same small group.

- Ask students to share their written work with their new partner.

VARIATION 2

- Repeat steps 1 through 7.

- Give each student two blank cards.

- Ask each student to draw or write something on each card.

- Ask each student to add his/her "homemade" cards to the table and explain them to the group.

Following Directions

Activity type: Free conversation

Time: 15-25 minutes

Number of players: Pairs

Materials: One scene card for each pair

PROCEDURE

1. Divide the class into pairs.

2. Give each pair a different scene card.

3. Write the following directions on the board:

   - Create a title for your picture.

   - Expand your picture by drawing a small addition.

   - Write three sentences describing your picture.

4. The first pair to correctly complete all three tasks is the winner.

5. Ask the winning pair to present their work to the class.

VARIATION 1

- Give students five tasks to complete.

- Make the tasks more complicated.

- After all the students have completed the tasks, collect the sentences.

- Use the sentences for additional grammar practice.

VARIATION 2

- Ask each pair to share their work with the class.

- Ask the class to vote on the best title and the best artist.

Creative Cards

Activity type: Free conversation

Time: 20 minutes

Number of players: Class

Materials: Seven enlarged scene cards

PROCEDURE

1. Choose, enlarge, and display seven scene cards.

2. Number them from one to seven.

3. Write the numbers one through seven on slips of paper and put them in a small box.

4. Give the class five minutes to walk up and quietly study the pictures.

5. After all the students have returned to their seats, have a volunteer pick a numbered slip from the small box.

6. Ask the volunteer student to do the following:

   - Keep the number a secret from the rest of the class.

   - Describe the corresponding picture in detail.

7. Ask the remainder of the class to listen and guess which picture is being described.

8. The first student to correctly guess draws the next number from the box and repeats the activity.

9. Continue until only one picture remains.

VARIATION 1

- Repeat steps 1 through 4.

- Choose a number slip from the box and describe in detail that picture for the class.

- After a student guesses correctly, repeat the activity.

- Continue until only one picture remains.

- As a class, write a detailed description of the one remaining picture.

VARIATION 2

- Repeat steps 1 through 9, EXCEPT for the following:

  - Divide the class into two equal teams.

  - Use 10 scene cards instead of seven.

  - Ask each team to describe and guess five of the cards.

  - Time each team's effort.

  - The team with the lowest cumulative time is the winner.

Going to the Moon!

Activity type: Free conversation

Time: 30 minutes

Number of players: Small groups

Materials: 10-15 miscellaneous object cards for each group of four

PROCEDURE

1. Divide the class into groups of four.

2. Give each group the same 10 to 15 object cards.

3. Read the situation.

4. Ask each group to do the following.

   - Discuss what they will need for the new colony.

   - Choose eight of the 15 things to take with them to the moon.

   - Be ready to explain WHY they chose what they did.

   - Appoint one spokesperson to share the group's choices and reasons with the class.

5. Share and discuss similarities and differences in the groups' choices.

Situation

In the year 2020 there will be a new settlement on the moon. Your group has been chosen to be included in the first group of settlers. There is very little space, so you can take only a few things with you. Choose carefully!

VARIATION 1

- Repeat steps 1 through 5.

- Ask each group to brainstorm additional items that would be necessary for survival.

- Share and discuss the students' ideas.

Creative Cards

Activity type: Free conversation

Time: 10-15 minutes

Number of players: Class

Materials: 10-12 FOOD object cards

PROCEDURE

1. Write the words *GOOD* and *BAD* on the board.

2. Show one food object card to the class.

3. Ask the class: "Is this food good for you or bad for you?"

4. Does everyone have the same opinion? Discuss students' opinions.

5. Repeat with a second food object card.

6. Continue for 10 minutes or until all the cards have been discussed.

7. Use this activity as an introduction to a unit on healthy eating habits or good nutrition.

VARIATION 1

- After the opening discussion, divide the class into groups of four.

- Ask each group to make its own lists of good and bad habits.

- Ask each group to present its ideas to the class.

VARIATION 2

- Do a debate on the pros and cons of a controversial health issue.

- Some possible topics are smoking, vegetarianism, or alternative medicine.

Impromptu

Activity type: Free conversation

Time: 20 minutes

Number of players: Class

Materials: One scene card for each student

PROCEDURE

1. Choose a variety of scene cards—you will need one for each student.

2. Put all the cards in a box and mix them up.

3. Randomly assign each student a number.

4. Ask student number one to choose one card from the box.

5. Ask student number one to talk for 30 seconds about the chosen card.

6. He/she may talk on any topic connected in some way with the picture. It is his/her choice.

7. After 30 seconds, ask student number two to pick a card and speak for 30 seconds.

8. Continue until all students have had a turn.

VARIATION 1

- Follow the same procedure, but do it in smaller groups. Smaller groups may be less threatening for shyer students.

VARIATION 2

- Repeat steps 1 through 8.

- Assign the students who are not speaking a listening task.

- Here are some suggested tasks:

   - Determine what is on the speaker's card.

   - Give the speaker one piece of constructive criticism.

   - Tell the speaker one thing he/she did well during the talk.

   - Be ready to ask the speaker one question at the conclusion of the talk.

Creative Cards

Activity type: Free conversation

Time: 10-15 minutes

Number of players: Pairs

Materials: Six scene cards for each pair

PROCEDURE

1. Divide the class into pairs.

2. Give each pair six scene cards.

3. Ask each pair to stack the cards face down in a pile on the table.

4. Read the following scenario as a class. Clarify meaning if necessary.

Situation

You are old friends who have not seen each other in several weeks. You run into each other at the grocery store and talk about what you have been doing.

5. Ask one partner in each pair to do the following:

   - Turn over the top card.

   - Use this card as a cue to explain what he/she has been doing.

   - Continue for one to two minutes.

6. After two minutes, ask the second partner to turn over the next card and continue the conversation.

7. Continue until all the cards have been discussed.

VARIATION 1

- Ask each pair to role-play one exchange for the class.

Categories

Activity type: Free conversation

Time: 15 minutes

Number of players: Class

Materials: The same 10 object cards (from several different themes) for each group

PROCEDURE

1. Divide the class into groups of four.

2. Give each group the same 10 object cards.

3. Ask each group to do the following:

   - Spread the cards on the table.

   - Discuss and agree upon three general categories.

   - Work together to categorize each of the 10 cards according to the agreed-upon categories.

   - Appoint a spokesperson.

   - Explain to the class which categories the group picked and why.

Example

These cards could be sorted by the categories Produce, Meat, and Dairy.

VARIATION 1

- Give beginning learners three categories and ask them to sort the cards accordingly.

VARIATION 2

- After each group has sorted its cards, ask them to change places with another group.

- Each group must then try to determine by which categories their classmates sorted the cards.

Creative Cards

Activity type: Free conversation

Time: 15-20 minutes (depending on class size)

Number of players: Class

Materials: A large selection of scene cards from different themes

PROCEDURE

1. Mix up all the cards and spread them out on a table.

2. Ask each student to do the following:

   - Choose one card that he/she thinks is beautiful.

   - Show the picture to the class.

   - Explain WHY he/she thinks it is beautiful.

3. Continue until each student has had a turn.

VARIATION 1

- Ask each student to choose two cards according to opposites.

- Some examples of selection criteria:

   - Beautiful/ugly

   - Fun/boring

   - Safe/dangerous

   - Likes/dislikes

VARIATION 2

- Display one enlarged scene card for the class.

- Ask all the students who like what's on the card to go to one side of the room.

- Ask the rest of the students to go to the other side of the room.

- Ask each group to come up with three reasons WHY they like/dislike the picture.

- Share ideas with the class.

- As in Variation 1, this can be done with several different adjective pairs.

3 . . . 2 . . . 1 . . . Action!

Activity type: Free conversation

Time: 30 minutes

Number of players: Pairs

Materials: One to five object cards for each pair

PROCEDURE

1. Choose one object card and make enough copies for each pair.

2. Choose two people who are connected with the object and write their identities on the board.

   Example: Object: Sandwich

              People: Waitress and Customer

3. Ask each pair to do the following:

   - Write a short conversation between two people.

   - Share their work with the class.

Hint

During free conversation periods, encourage students to focus on communication rather than grammatical accuracy.

VARIATION 1

- Choose one theme.

- Give each pair any two object cards from that theme.

- Ask each pair to do the following:

  - Choose two people who are connected with the object.

  Example: Object: Airplane

             People: Flight Attendant and Passenger

  - Create a role-play (three to four exchanges).

  - Perform the role-play.

VARIATION 2

- Give each pair any three object cards.

- Ask each pair to do the following:

  - Create a role-play incorporating all three objects (five to six exchanges).

  - Perform the role-play.

- Following each performance, ask the rest of the class to guess what the objects were.

Animals

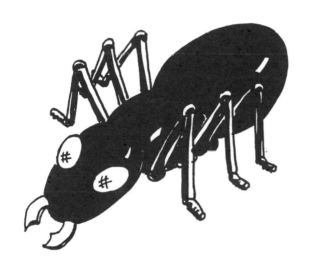

Animals

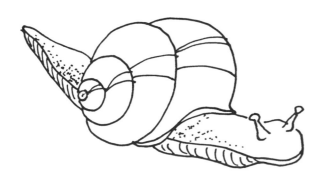

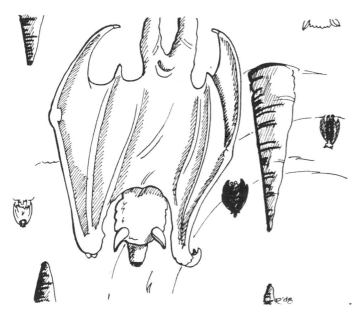

Clothes

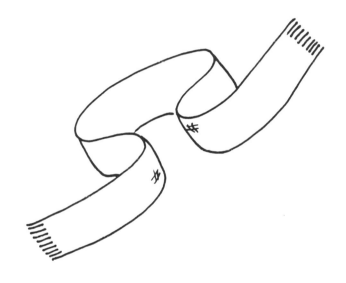

Clothes

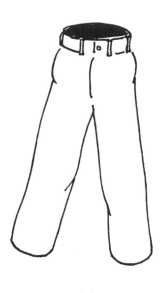

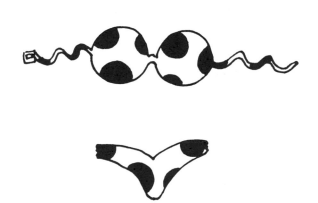

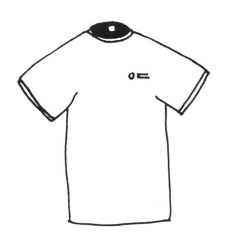

Clothes

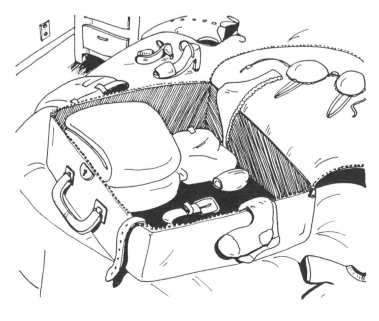

Environment

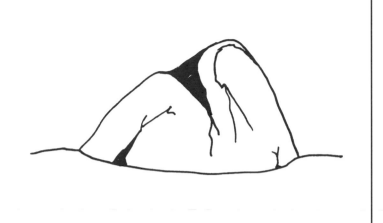

Environment

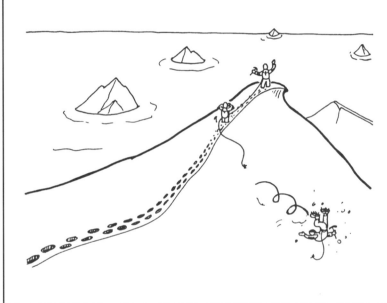

Food

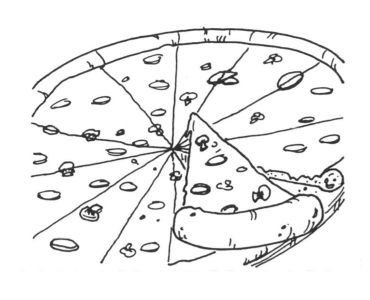
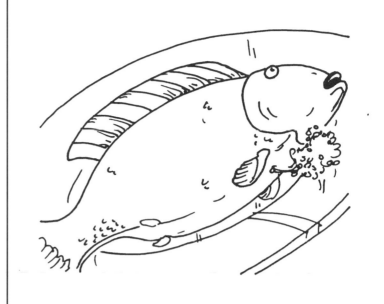
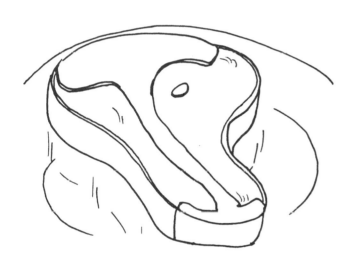
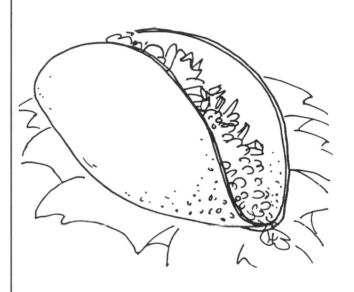
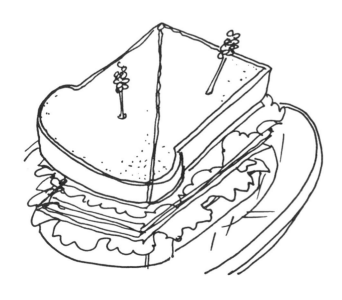

Food

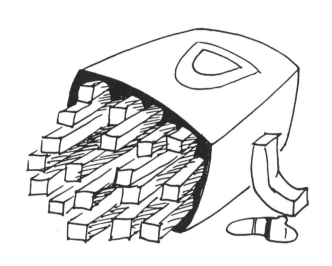
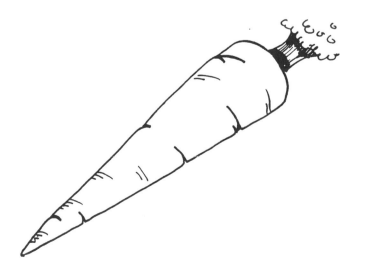

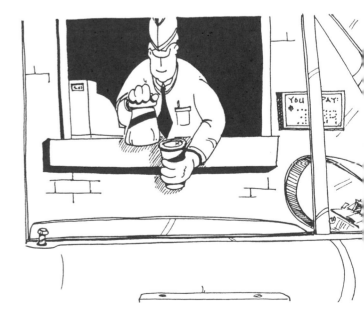

Health

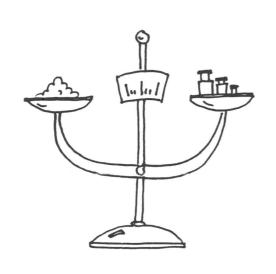

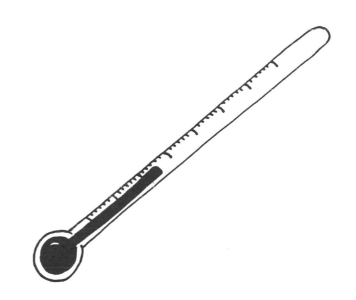

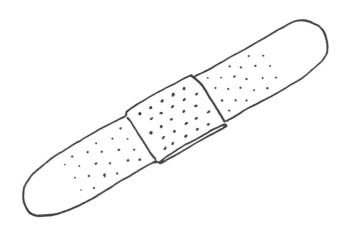

Health

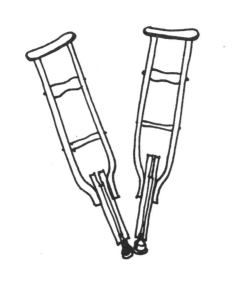

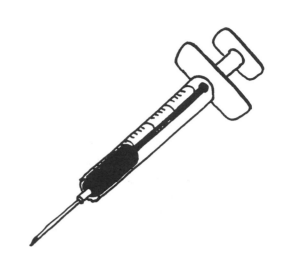

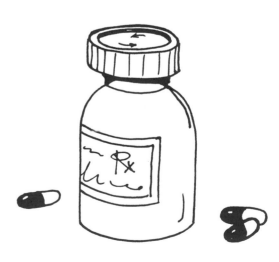

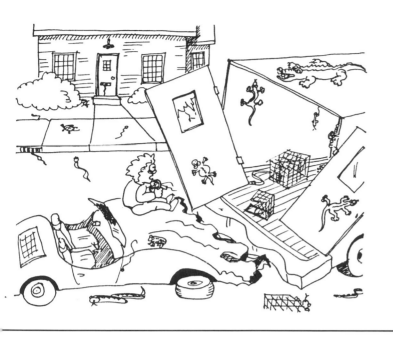

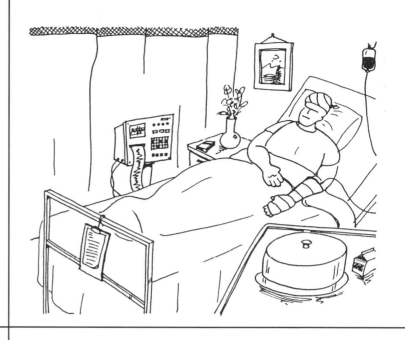

Welcome to
SHADY ACRES REST HOME

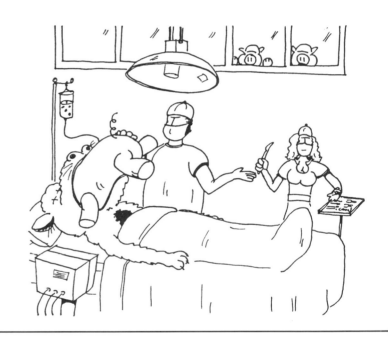

Holidays

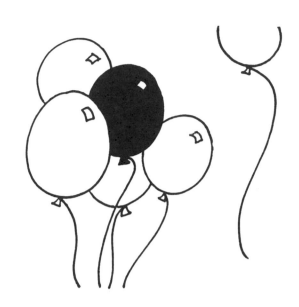

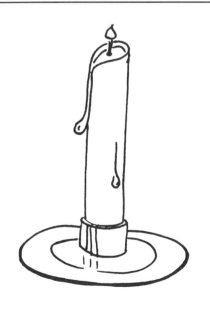

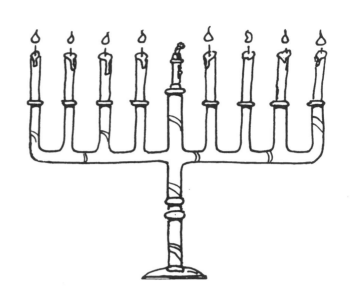

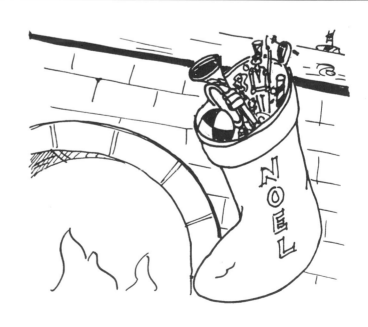

Occupations

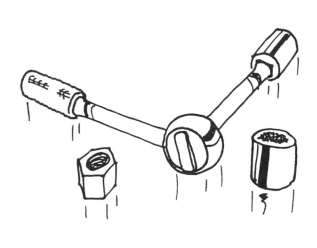

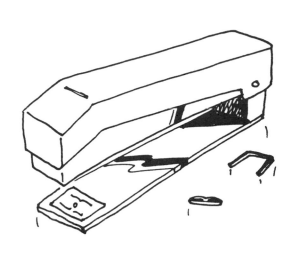

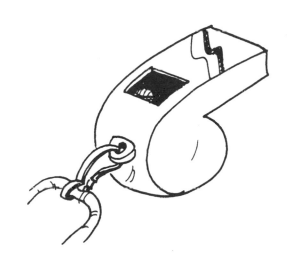

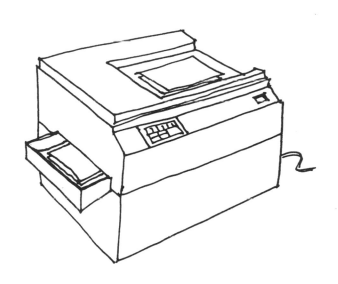

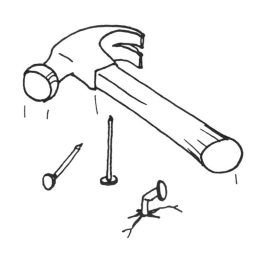

Occupations

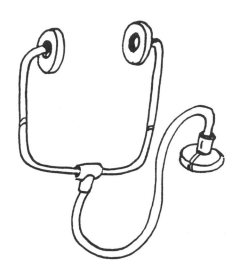

Occupations

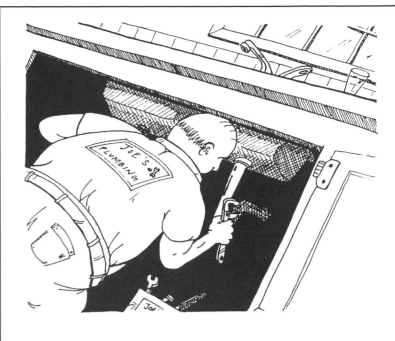

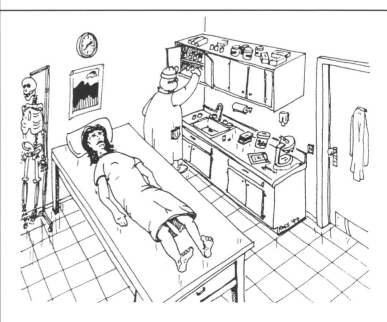

Occupations

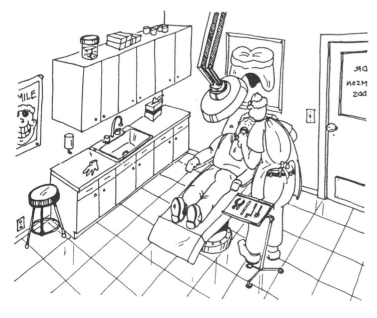

People

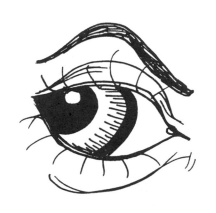

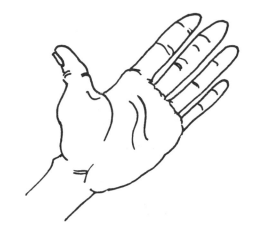

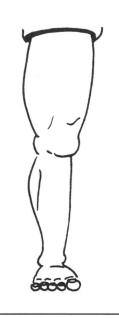

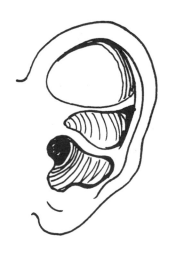

People

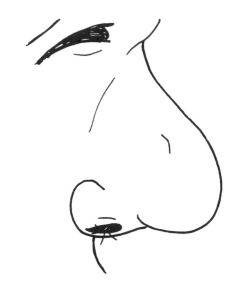

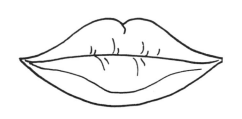

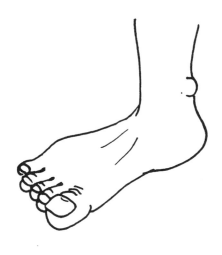

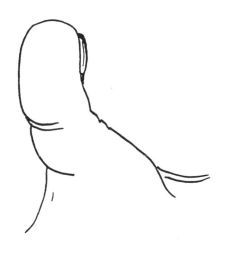

School

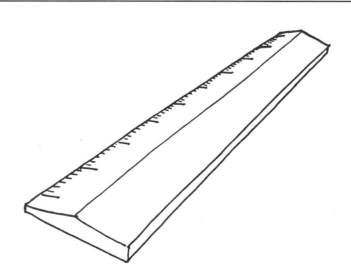

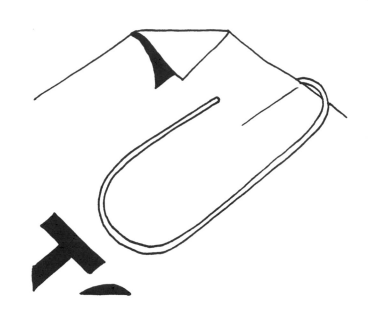

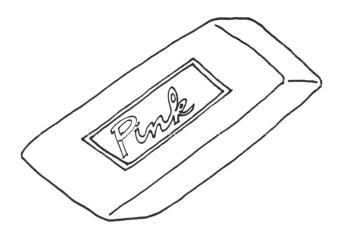

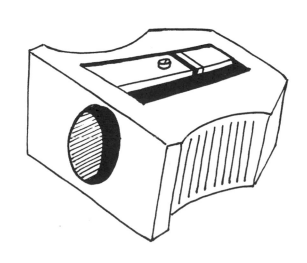

Sports

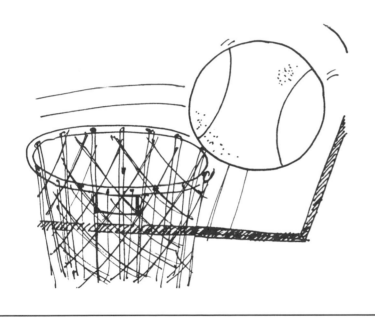

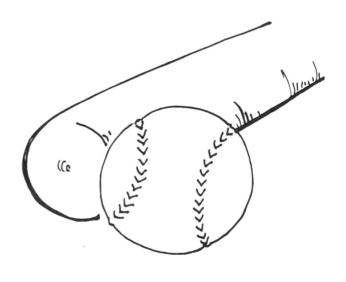

Sports

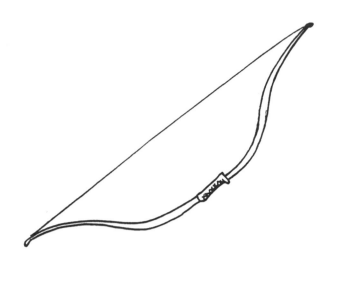

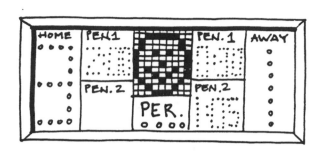

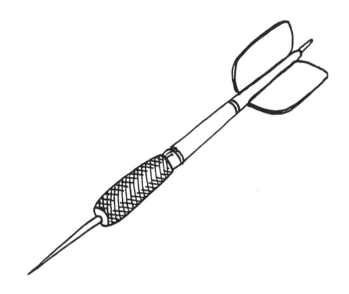

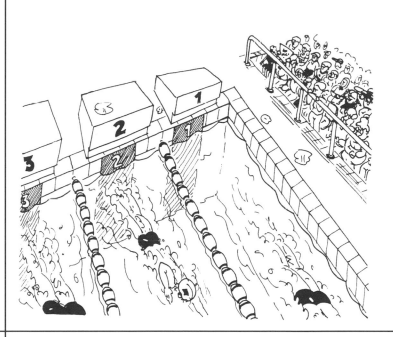

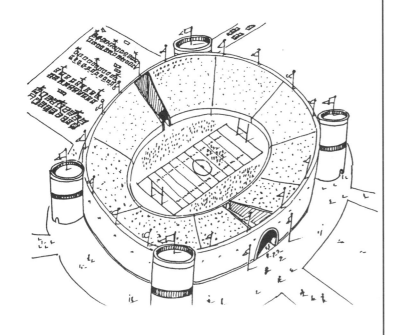

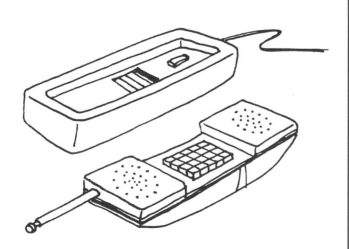

Technology

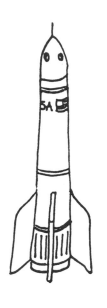

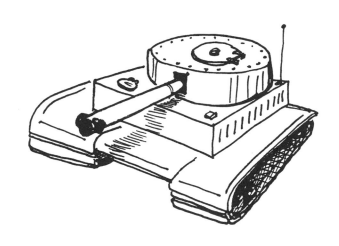

Technology

Transportation

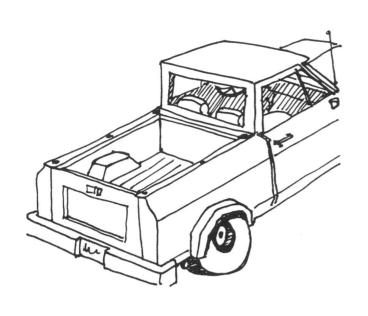

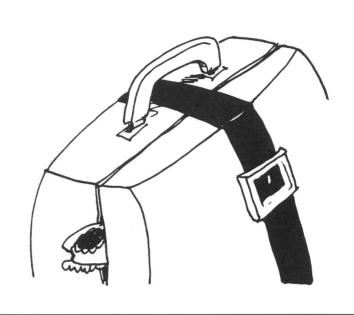

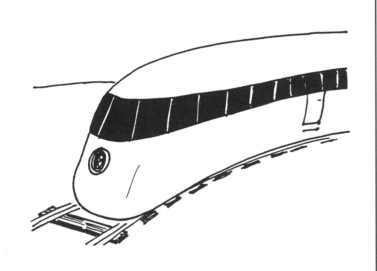

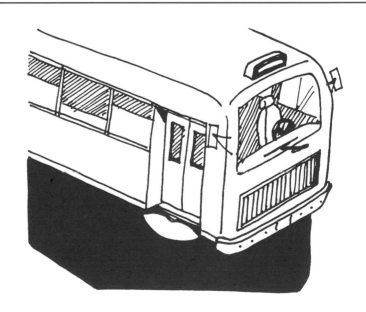

Transportation

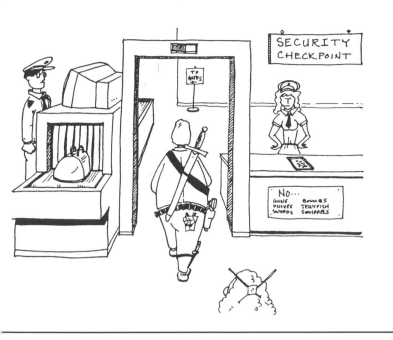

Creative Cards

Creative Cards

Creative Cards

Appendix 4: Skill Area Index

Creative Cards

Creative Cards

ANIMALS

moose in the wild
birds at feeder
kittens playing
horses in a pasture
bat in a cave
mother pig with piglets
zoo bears
barnyard
lily pad frog
jumping fish
family dog by the fire
circus elephant

CLOTHING

at the beach
clothes closet
in the shoe store
shopping in the baby department
packing for a trip
baby wearing daddy's boots
man exercising
man in pajamas
a bride and groom
shopping in the hat store
fashion show
playing in the snow

ENVIRONMENT

in the woods
at the river
in the desert
at a waterfall
at the lake
deep sea life
man hiking in the mountains
factory and nature
in the meadow
on the mountain
recycling center
in the jungle

OCCUPATIONS

farmer in the fields
housepainter at work
bartender at work
judge on the bench
dentist office
artist's studio
working at the computer
working plumber
teaching music
driving a bus
policeman on duty
hospital exam room

PEOPLE

husband and wife
old woman in a rocker
two women having tea
boy riding a bike
woman jogging
old man feeding birds
toddler in a highchair
girl playing with dolls
two men fishing
baby in a playpen
man at a casino
man surfing

SCHOOL

homework
at band practice
teacher in front of class
empty classroom
bulletin board
school building
waiting for principal
in the science lab
child studying
students in a class
in the gym
playground equipment

FOOD

cooking at the stove
romantic dinner
open refrigerator
in the diner
supermarket check out
fast-food drive thru
eating by TV
a kitchen
family dinner
fast-food cashier
summer picnic
at the deli

HEALTH

car accident
in the hospital
working out
drinking beer
wheelchair race
ambulance incident
immunizations
bowl of fruit
poisons under sink
in the operating room
smoking and exercising
boy with scraped elbow

HOLIDAYS

Christmas tree with gifts
mother's day sale
Valentine's Day
Easter bunny
baby's first birthday
opening gifts
a parade
Thanksgiving dinner
New Year's eve party
Santa Claus
trick or treating

SPORTS

playing darts in a bar
playing golf
referee in action
scuba diving
sports stadium
playing volleyball
horse jumping
playing soccer
downhill skiing
swim meet
fishing in the country
playing baseball

TECHNOLOGY

video games
dismantled car engine
computer frustration
space shuttle
remote control TV
factory assembly line
a UFO
cave man and a satellite dish
working on a laptop
using a cell phone
busy office
video taping family life

TRANSPORTATION & TRAVEL

airport security
riding on a train
airplane problems
going on a cruise
airline waiting area
backpacking
traffic jam
stuck in the mud
at the train station
out of gas
sailing fun
getting in a taxi

Creative Cards

A
american flag
airplane
ant
apple

B
baby
backpack
balloons
banana
bandage
baseball
basket
basketball
bathrobe
bicycle
bikini
bird
boat
book
boot
bow (and arrow)
bus
butterfly

C
cactus
cake
calculator
candle
candy
car
carrot
cat
celery
Christmas stocking
cigarette
clock
clouds
computer
copy machine
cow
crocodile
crutches

E
ear
egg
eraser
eye

F
face
fish
flower
flower bouquet
foot
football helmet
french fries
frog

G
gift
girl
glue bottle
golf club
grapes
gun

H
hamburger
hammer
hand
hat
hockey skate
hockey stick

J
jacket
jack-o-lantern

L
ladder
leaf
leg
lightbulb
lion
lips
locker

M
medicine bottle
menorah
microwave oven
mop
motorcycle
mountain

N
nose
notebook
nurse

O
oak tree
old man

P
palm tree
pants
paperclip
pen
pencil
pencil sharpener
pizza
plant

R
robot
rock
rocket
ruler

S
salad
sandwich
scale
scarf
scoreboard
sheep
shoe
shovel
ski
snail

snow machine
soccer ball
sock
spider
stapler
steak
stethoscope
stone
suitcase
sun
syringe

T
t-shirt
taco
tank
telephone
telephone pole
television
tennis racket
thermometer
thumb
tie
train
tree
truck--pickup
truck--semi
typewriter

V
video camera
video cassette recorder
volcano

W
wheelchair
whistle
wreath

Creative Cards

Creative Cards 115

Clark, RL. (1993). *More Index Card Games and activities for English:.* Brattleboro, VT: Pro Lingua Associates.

Holt, Grace, and Massey. (1995). *Teaching low-level adult ESL learners.* ERIC digest.

Kippel, F. (1984). *Keep talking: communicative fluency activities for language teaching.* Cambridge: Cambridge University Press.

Morgan, J. and Rinvolucri, M. (1983). *Once Upon a Time: Using stories in the language classroom.* Cambridge: Cambridge University Press.

Richard-Amato, P. A. (1988). *Making it happen: Interaction in the second language classroom: from theory to practice.* White Plains, NY: Longman.

Schmidt, K. (Jan. 1995). *Optimizing picture activities for the language classroom: Picture line-up activities.* Language Teaching: The Korea TESOL Journal; v.2 n.4, 102-108.

Sanders, K. (1998). *The Interactive Tutorial: An Activity Parade.* Brattleboro, VT: Pro Lingua Associates.

Tom, A. and McKay, H. (1991). *The Card Book.* Englewood Cliffs, NJ: Alemany Press.

Ur,P. (1988). *Grammar practice activities.* Cambridge: Cambridge University Press.

Winn-Bell Olsen, J. (1984). *Look Again Pictures.* Englewood Cliffs, NJ: Alemany Press.

Wright,A. (1989). *Pictures for language learning.* Cambridge: Cambridge University Press.